JUDAISM'S GREAT DEBATES

Teacher's Lesson Plan Manual
By Rachael Gelfman Schultz

24 Ready-to-Use Lesson Plans

Project Editor: Mark H. Levine
Design: Annemarie Redmond
Copyright © Behrman House, Inc.
Springfield, New Jersey
ISBN: 978-0-87441-853-8 • Manufactured in the United States of America

Behrman House, Inc.
www.behrmanhouse.com
www.behrmanhouse.com/greatdebates

Contents

Introduction

Judaism's Great Debates invites students to explore great debates of Jewish history and the eternal value conflicts that lie at the heart of those debates, while applying those value conflicts to contemporary challenges.

STRUCTURE OF THE TEXTBOOK

The book has ten chapters, each of which centers around a great debate in Jewish history and the underlying value conflict. Chapters include the following recurring features:

- **Opening Vignette:** Historical and intellectual context for the Great Debate.

- **History Timeline:** Major events that provide context for the Great Debate.

- **Clarification Questions:** Thought-provoking discussion questions on the introductory vignette and history timeline.

- **The Great Debate:** A mix of fictional dialogue and historic sources (which appear in italics), such as the Tanach, Midrash, letters and books written by the debaters, communal archives, and eye-witness accounts.

- **Cross Examination:** Discussion questions which help students to process the Great Debate.

- **Competing Values:** Two conflicting Jewish values (in Hebrew with English translations) that are at the heart of each debate.

- **Debate It:** Contemporary challenge that shares the same value conflict as the Great Debate.

- **Reflections:** Exploratory questions that help students internalize the values and take action.

- **Echoes from the Past:** A contemporary or historical figure who takes action on the values to create social change.

- **What Would You Do?** A modern-day fictional case that challenges the student to decide where he or she stands on the values conflict.

VALUES CONFLICT DEBATE

The debates in this book are Lincoln-Douglas debates, meaning that the arguments are focused on the underlying values conflict. Lincoln-Douglas debates are structured around a "resolution," the debate term for a topic of discussion that is centered on a values conflict. Resolutions are stated as if one side of the dilemma is correct. During the debate, the affirmative side argues that the resolution is correct, and the negative side argues that it is incorrect. For instructions on how to organize a Lincoln-Douglas values conflict debate, tips on building an effective argument, and analysis of each resolution, see www.behrmanhouse.com/greatdebates.

STRUCTURE OF THIS LESSON PLAN MANUAL

This Lesson Plan Manual presents 24 ready-to-use lesson plans of approximately 45-50 minutes each for *Judaism's Great Debates*. It includes suggestions for teaching every element of the student text. The introduction includes an overview of experiential learning, and each lesson incorporates an experiential learning component. In addition, ideas on how to incorporate technology are included in many lessons.

Each lesson plan includes:

- **Essential Question:** An overarching question, one that we may ask at different times in our lives, that reflects the main idea of the lesson.

- **Lesson Objectives:** Specific goals for each lesson that correspond to the concepts and ideas that students should understand when they complete the lesson.

- **Getting Started:** A set induction to get students thinking about the ideas they will learn in that lesson.

- **Exploring the Text:** A step-by-step guide for presenting the lesson, including suggested questions and activities and the approximate time for each segment of the lesson.

- **Wrapping It Up:** A short activity or discussion to review and reflect on the main ideas presented in the lesson.

EXPERIENTIAL LEARNING

Each lesson plan also includes suggestions for experiential learning. Many students learn best by doing. As the ancient Chinese philosopher Confucius said: "Tell me and I will forget, show me and I may remember, involve me and I will understand." The activities suggested range from creating artwork, to performing a skit, to planning and executing social justice and *chesed* projects. Whenever your class learns through direct experience, it is important for your students to reflect on their experience at the end of the activity or lesson. What did I learn from this activity? How does it deepen my understanding of the Jewish values we are studying? What questions does this experience raise for me?

USING THIS LESSON PLAN MANUAL

At the start of the year, map out when you plan to teach each chapter. The 24 lessons in the manual have been designed so that you can teach an average of one lesson a week.

Before you begin to teach a textbook chapter, read through the Lesson Plan Manual to familiarize yourself with the chapter. You may choose to use the lessons exactly as they are, or you may adapt the lessons to fit the needs of your students. If you adapt the lessons, it is important to frame your lesson around an essential question — either the one suggested for the lesson or another one that points to the main idea of the lesson.

BEING INCLUSIVE

Children vary in their learning styles. Some students learn best with a hands-on approach, while others do best with a visual or an auditory approach. In general, teachers who present material in many different ways will be able to reach many more children.

Teachers of children with special needs have extra challenges. These children may have a broad range of cognitive, physical, and behavioral disabilities that impact learning. It is always helpful to find out from parents what accommodations are made for their child in secular school. The suggestions included below are primarily for those children with learning, perceptual, or attention problems.

- For students with attention and auditory processing problems, teach in small increments and present one instruction at a time. Ask the children to repeat the instruction to be sure they have processed it.

- For children with attention problems, limit teaching segments to 10 to 15 minutes and allow for movement between activities.

- For children with decoding problems, make flash cards with a few key words. Children can take them home and practice reading them with their parents. Keep a shoe box of flash cards for children who need them. Provide opportunities for choral reading rather than asking children to read aloud individually.

- For children with attention and visual figure-ground problems, mask parts of the page so they can see only the section that is being worked on.

- For children with fine motor and handwriting problems, limit the amount of writing, drawing, and cutting that is required. Prepare these difficult parts of a project in advance of the class and have students finish the task. This is an excellent way to engage a classroom *madrich* or *madrichah*. (*The Madrichim Manual* (Behrman House) is an excellent resource for learning how to engage *madrichim* appropriately.)

Remember, the relationships that you build with the students and that you help them build with one another are as important as the material you teach. Consistently try to model patience and respect for all students.

INTERPERSONAL AND INTRAPERSONAL LEARNERS

Some students learn best through interacting with others (interpersonal); some learn best independently (intrapersonal). With this in mind, there are suggestions in the lesson plans for independent work and for activities and discussions with a partner, group, or the whole class. In general, if the manual does not specify that students are meeting with a partner or in a group, plan to have a class discussion.

GROUP WORK

Many of the lessons include suggestions for group work. Whenever possible, plan ahead how you want to form the groups. It is important to change the composition of your groups. For some tasks you will want students with a variety of talents and interests. For others you may choose to group together students with similar skills.

Group work is most successful when every group member knows his or her responsibilities. To help make the group's task clear, prepare written instructions before the class. Many of the lesson plans include such instructions.

Consider creating index cards that describe the jobs of group members. Jobs will vary depending on the type of group work. Some possible jobs include the following:

- Recorder—records the group's suggestions or findings that will be reported to the class
- Reporter—reports the group's work to the class
- Illustrator—draws the group's ideas to be presented to the class
- Investigator—researches to discover information
- Encourager—encourages group members to stay on task
- Reader—reads aloud information to the group

Consider laminating the job description index cards and distributing them each time you do group work.

USING TECHNOLOGY

Your students are growing up in a world in which technology is part of their daily lives at home and at school. There are infinite ways that you can take advantage of the Internet and digital applications to deepen understanding, reinforce concepts, share learning with families, and add creativity, interactivity, and excitement to your lessons.

With your students, visit www.behrmanhouse.com/greatdebates. The site provides valuable resources that will enrich and deepen your students' learning. The historic debaters featured in each chapter are profiled in depth, including pictures, biographies, links to key resources about the character, and central questions answered by the character. The website provides links to multimedia resources and resources that will help students prepare for the debate, answer the reflection questions raised in the text, and implement the values raised in the debate. The website also includes additional texts for each of the competing values.

Introduction, Lesson 1

Essential Question: What is machloket l'shem shamayim and how can we apply this value in our classroom?

Lesson Objectives: Students will be able to:

Explain why debate is so central to the Jewish tradition.

Define *machloket l'shem shamayim.*

Formulate guidelines for how to debate respectfully.

Getting Started: (10 minutes)

Students walk randomly around the room. When the teacher says stop, students turn to the person closest to them and decide which person is A and which is B. The teacher gives a topic to debate, and says which side A will argue and which side B will argue. Students debate the topic for one minute. Topics of debate should be fun and relevant to your particular group of students. Examples could include: Coke vs. Pepsi, Mets vs. Yankees, or hamantashen vs. latkes. Repeat the exercise several times. Each time, students walk around the room, find a different partner, and debate a different topic. Sometimes, switch which student is A and which student is B without switching partners or topics. When you are done, explain that this class is going to be all about debates: debates in Jewish history, debates in our society today, and the connection between the two.

Exploring the Text:

1. (10 minutes) Students act out the story in the beginning of the introduction, playing the parts of the narrator, Rabbi Eliezer, the sages, Rabbi Joshua, and God. A group of students stands silently behind the speakers and uses movement to represent the carob tree, the stream of water, and the walls of the schoolhouse.

2. (5 minutes) Discuss: What does Rabbi Joshua mean when he says that: "The answer is not from Heaven?" What does God mean when He says that "My children have defeated me?" Why is God happy about being defeated? What is the message of the story? What does the story tell us about the importance of debate in the Jewish tradition?

3. (5 minutes) In pairs, read "The Spirit of Jewish Debate" and "Debate for the Sake of Heaven" and define *machloket l'shem shamayim.*

4. (15 minutes) **Experiential Learning:** On a posterboard, write at the top *Machloket L'Shem Shamayim: Our Classroom Guidelines.* As a class, write a list of guidelines for debate in your classroom that are in keeping with the principle of *machloket l'shem shamayim (do not speak when someone else is speaking, do not make fun of someone else's opinion, encourage those who have not spoken yet to express their opinions …).* Place the poster in a prominent place in your classroom where the students or teacher can refer to it throughout the course whenever someone needs a reminder of how to debate respectfully.

Wrapping It Up: (5 minutes)

Read the rest of the introduction together as a class, and make sure the students understand how each chapter is structured. Emphasize that each chapter explores a value conflict that is at the core of the historical debate and is relevant to our lives today.

Abraham and God, Lesson 1

Essential Question: Is collective punishment just?

Lesson Objectives: Students will be able to:

1. Make arguments for and against collective punishment.

2. Explain why Abraham confronts God regarding Sodom and Gomorrah.

3. Define tzedakah and *mishpat* and explain how these values may conflict.

Getting Started: (5 minutes)

Present the following scenario to the students: Several students in your class are misbehaving, so the next day, the teacher punishes the entire class by giving a difficult pop quiz on the material from the previous day. Like many people, you fail the quiz, even though you were paying attention in class. You are upset—you were not one of the students misbehaving! Was it fair of the teacher to give a pop quiz to the entire class when not everyone was misbehaving? With a show of hands, students vote on whether the pop quiz was fair or not. Students defend each position.

Exploring the Text:

1. (5 minutes) Student reads the introduction out loud. Discuss: Was God's decision to destroy Sodom and Gomorrah just? Note that both God destroying all of Sodom and Gomorrah, and the teacher giving the entire class a pop quiz, are collective punishment. The entire group is punished even though only some of the people in the group are guilty. Is collective punishment ever just? When?

2. (15 minutes) In pairs, read Genesis 6:13 - 7:5. How is Noah's reaction to God's decision to destroy the world different than Abraham's reaction to God's decision to destroy Sodom and Gomorrah? Why? Each person in the pair answers the question: If you were Abraham, would you have confronted God? Or would you have remained silent, like Noah? Why?

3. (10 minutes) **Experiential Learning:** Before looking at the script, two students go to the front of the classroom and act out what they imagine the debate between Abraham and God was like. Students should think about *what* arguments each side would make, and *how* each side would present their arguments (language, tone of voice, gestures). At any point, a student from the audience may go to the front of the room and replace one of the students playing Abraham or God, either to make a new argument or to change the tone of the argument.

4. (5 minutes) Two students then act out the scripted debate. Ask: What arguments does Abraham make, in your own words? What is his tone in approaching God?

Wrapping It Up: (5 minutes)

Write the words *mishpat* and tzedakah on two sides of the blackboard and translate them. Ask: Which of Abraham's arguments fall under the category of *mishpat*, and which fall under the category of tzedakah? Write the arguments under the proper heading. Do you agree with Abraham's arguments for *mishpat* or for tzedakah or both? Why or why not?

Abraham and God, Lesson 2

Essential Question: How should we balance justice and compassion in our lives and in our society?

Lesson Objectives: Students will be able to:

1. Provide real life examples of people acting on *mishpat* or tzedakah.

2. Discuss how and why *mishpat* and tzedakah conflict in our society.

3. Design projects that will help realize the values of *mishpat* and tzedakah in our community.

Getting Started: (5 minutes)

Write *mishpat* and tzedakah on the board. Students brainstorm examples from their lives, in history, or in current events where someone was either compassionate or demanded justice. Write the examples under the proper heading.

Exploring the Text:

1. (10 minutes) Each student privately does the following writing exercise: Do you tend to be more compassionate or demand justice? Are there times in your life when you should be more compassionate or more assertive in demanding justice? When? What prevents you from being compassionate or demanding justice? What steps can you take to overcome those obstacles? What do you learn from Abraham about being compassionate and demanding justice?

2. (5 minutes) Explain that in the U.S. criminal justice system, *mishpat* and tzedakah often come into conflict when deciding how to punish the criminal. One student reads the paragraph called "Debate It," and another student reads "Echoes from the Past."

3. (5 minutes) In pairs, debate the question: Do you agree with prison reforms designed to help rehabilitate criminals to become contributing members of society? Why or why not? What are the advantages and drawbacks of such reforms? (*Advantages: when released from prison, prisoners less likely to return to life of crime; drawbacks: more expensive, people may be more likely to commit crimes if they know that life in prison is not all that bad*)

4. (20 minutes) **Experiential Learning:** Divide the class into small groups. Each small group plans either a tzedakah project or a social justice (*mishpat*) project that the group can work on over the next several weeks. Ideas for tzedakah projects include a food, clothing, or book drive for people in need in your community, or volunteering as a group in your local soup kitchen. Ideas for social justice projects include writing a petition to government officials (such as for prison reform) or a boycott of companies that treat their workers unfairly. Students may use the Internet to research their project.

Wrapping It Up: (5 minutes)

Students reflect with the class: How did your group decide on a project? Did you focus on tzedakah or *mishpat*? Why? Whom will your project benefit? Why was it important to you to help these people?

Moses and Korach, Lesson 1

Essential Question: What makes a good leader?

Lesson Objectives: Students will be able to:

1. Describe what makes a good leader.

2. Evaluate whether Moses was a good leader in the way he responded to the people's complaints, and particularly to Korach.

3. Define the terms *manhigut* and *kavod habriyot* and explain the connection between them.

Getting Started: (5 minutes)

Brainstorm with the class: What qualities do you look for in a leader? List the qualities on the board.

Exploring the Text:

1. (15 minutes) **Experiential Learning:** Each student chooses one of his or her favorite leaders and makes a page on the computer describing the leader and what he or she admires about that leader. The pages will be put together as an online gallery of leaders. When students finish, they can go around the room and look at other students' work.

2. (5 minutes) In pairs, students share their work and identify the qualities they admire in the leader they chose.

3. (5 minutes) Students read the introduction and timeline together and discuss: How would you respond to each rebellion if you were Moses? How do good leaders respond to their people's complaints?

4. (10 minutes) Students split into groups of four and read the debate together, with students playing Moses, Korach, and Datan and Aviram. Each group answers the question: How does Moses respond to Korach, Datan, and Aviram?

5. (5 minutes) Gather the class together. Write the terms *manhigut* and *kavod habriyot* on the board, and translate them. Discuss: Was Moses a good leader (*manhigut*) in this situation? Why or why not? Did Moses show *kavod habriyot* in his interaction with Korach and Datan and Aviram? What is the connection between *kavod habriyot* and good leadership?

Wrapping It Up: (5 minutes)

Students write the answers to the second and third reflection questions privately. Which qualities do you share with the leaders you admire (including Moses)? How can you improve your leadership skills?

Moses and Korach, Lesson 2

Essential Question: Should the power to lead a community be limited to a few people who are best suited to be leaders, or should that power be shared among as many people as possible?

Lesson Objectives: Students will be able to:

1. Explain Korach's argument that the entire community should be priests.

2. Discuss the advantages and disadvantages of elitism.

3. Examine situations in their own lives where power is limited to one or a few individuals and evaluate whether the leadership model works in those situations.

Getting Started: (5 minutes)

Write the quote on the board: "For all the community are holy, every one of them, and God is in their midst. Why then do you raise yourselves above God's congregation?" (Korach to Moses, Numbers 16:3). What is Korach's argument? Do you agree? Why or why not? Explain the term elitism.

Exploring the Text:

1. (5 minutes) In pairs, answer the questions in "Cross Examination."

2. (10 minutes) A student reads "What Would You Do?" Students prepare to act out the meeting of the neighborhood club when they discuss the new committee for choosing members. Divide the students into two groups, the first group in favor of the new membership committee, and the second group opposed. Each group prepares a brief argument for its position, and a rebuttal of the other group's position.

3. (10 minutes) **Experiential Learning:** Act out the meeting. After each side presents its position, each side has an opportunity for a rebuttal.

4. (5 minutes) After the presentations and rebuttals, students express their own positions on the topic. Students may also suggest alternative methods of choosing new members. Students vote on whether or not to accept the new membership committee, the status quo, or an alternative method of choosing new members.

5. (5 minutes) Discuss: Think of people in authority positions in your life (*school principal, teacher, parent, athletic team coach*). Why are these people given authority? (*intelligence, life experience, university degrees, moral superiority*) Do you think that in these situations, it is good for one or two people to have most of the power, or would the school/classroom/family/sports team benefit from power being more democratically distributed? Why?

Wrapping It Up: (5 minutes)

In pairs, share a situation in which you felt like Korach, resentful of people who had power over you and frustrated that your own power was limited (*your teacher was running the class in a way you didn't like, your parents made a decision for you that you didn't agree with, etc.*) How did you respond? Were you able to improve the situation? Why or why not? Could you have responded in a more helpful way?

The Five Daughters and the Twelve Tribes, Lesson 1

Essential Question: How have women throughout Jewish history challenged women's status in their society?

Lesson Objectives: Students will be able to:

1. Provide examples of women in Jewish history who challenged women's status in their society.

2. Explain why Zelophehad's daughters challenged the biblical inheritance law.

3. Evaluate the competing arguments of Zelophehad's daughters and the tribal leaders.

Getting Started: (5 minutes)

Ask students: Is there anything you would change about women's status in the Jewish community you belong to? What? Explain that today we will look at Jewish women throughout history who challenged women's status in their community, focusing on the biblical story of Zelophehad's daughters.

Exploring the Text:

1. (15 minutes) **Experiential Learning**: Each student chooses a woman in Jewish history who challenged the status quo regarding women in her society. She may have done so publicly (*such as by being an outspoken female leader*) or privately (*such as by challenging her husband's decision within the family*); by something she said, or by something she did. Students may use the Internet to research the woman s/he chose. Students may also choose to write about a woman they know, a relative or a friend, in which case they may wish to interview the woman. Each student writes a poem, draws a picture, creates a one-page PowerPoint, or otherwise creatively represents the woman s/he chose, including how that woman challenged the status quo. Students can look at "Echoes from the Past" as an example of one such Jewish woman. Students display their work in the school to educate other students about these women's accomplishments.

2. (10 minutes) Students share their work in small groups. Each student answers the question: Why do you think this woman challenged the status quo? What risks did she take in doing so?

3. (5 minutes) Gather the class together and read the introduction. Discuss question #1 in "Clarification."

4. (10 minutes) Act out the debate, with students playing Zelophehad's daughters, Moses, God, and the tribal leaders. Ask: What was the compromise reached between Zelophehad's daughters and the tribal leaders? Was it just?

Wrapping It Up: (5 minutes)

In pairs, answer the following question: What would you do if you were Zelophehad's daughters? Would you challenge the biblical inheritance law? Why or why not? If yes, how would you challenge the law? Look at questions #1 and #2 in "Cross Examination" for additional factors to consider in making your decision.

The Five Daughters and the Twelve Tribes, Lesson 2

Essential Question: How can we strengthen our community while respecting each individual within it?

Lesson Objectives: Students will be able to:

1. Define the values *kehilah* and *b'tzelem Elohim* and explain how these two values can conflict.

2. Provide real life examples where these two values conflict.

3. Explore ways of balancing these two values historically and in their own lives.

Getting Started: (5 minutes)

Think back to the discussion at the beginning of the last class. Why do you think the changes in women's status that you discussed have not yet been made? What arguments could be made against them? How could preserving the status quo be good for your community? *(Some would argue that changing women's roles undermines tradition, which is a core value of the Jewish community).* Explain that today, we will look at situations in which an individual's rights conflict with communal values or welfare.

Exploring the Text:

1. (5 minutes) Write the words *"kehilah"* and *"b'tzelem Elohim"* on the board and translate them. How do these two values come into conflict in the case of Zelophehad's daughters? How are the changes in the inheritance laws that Zelophehad's daughters request good or bad for the community, and how do they protect or violate individual rights? How does the tribal leaders' argument appeal to the values of *kehilah* and/or *b'tzelem Elohim?*

2. (10 minutes) A student reads the paragraph "Debate It." Students prepare to debate whether children of undocumented workers are entitled to public education. Working individually, half of the students prepare arguments in favor, and half against. Students may use the Internet to prepare their arguments, researching the question of illegal immigration in the United States.

3. (5 minutes) In pairs, students debate the question of public education for children of undocumented workers, with one student arguing in favor and one arguing against.

4. (5 minutes) Gather the students. Ask: How would public education for these children be good or bad for the community? How would it protect or violate individual rights? Then vote on the question.

continues...

The Five Daughters and the Twelve Tribes, Lesson 2, continued

5. (15 minutes) **Experiential Learning:** Students choose a class project designed to make their community more welcoming and respectful of many different kinds of individuals. How can we balance *kehilah* and *b'tzelem Elohim* in our communities, as God and Moses did in the case of Zelophehad's daughters? Ideas may include:

   - Setting up a buddy system to welcome new students to the school.
   - Speaking to the rabbi/board members and raising money to make the synagogue more handicapped accessible, such as by building a ramp where necessary.
   - Buying Braille prayerbooks for the synagogue, or prayerbooks that include a translation in a language other than English if your community includes individuals who have difficulty with English.
   - Creating a scholarship fund to help families who are struggling financially to send their children to Hebrew school.

Wrapping It Up: (5 minutes)

Students complete the following writing exercise: Describe a time when you were happy to be part of the Jewish community and felt a strong sense of belonging, or describe a time when it was very difficult for you to be part of the Jewish community. What do you gain by joining the Jewish community? What do you lose? Do you have to give up any of your individual desires to join the community?

David and Nathan, Lesson 1

Essential Question: How can we give criticism that will be helpful rather than harmful?

Lesson Objectives: Students will be able to:

1. Provide examples of how to give helpful criticism (and how not to).

2. Describe how Nathan was able to give David criticism that would help him.

3. Define *ometz lev* and *lo talech rachil b'amecha* and explain how Nathan demonstrated these values in confronting David.

Getting Started: (5 minutes)

Give the students the following scenario: Your close friend Becky has started to sneak out of the house at night, and you are worried about her. You want to confront her, but you are not sure how to do so in a way that she will listen to you and possibly begin to change her ways. You also do not want to lose her friendship. How do you confront Becky? What do you say to her and how do you say it?

Each student writes down how s/he would confront Becky.

Exploring the Text:

1. (10 minutes) **Experiential Learning:** Two students come to the front of the classroom and act out the confrontation between the friend and Becky. Then, invite other pairs of students to act out different ways of confronting Becky. After the pairs have finished, students discuss what the friend said that was helpful to Becky, and what the friend said that could have hurt Becky or their relationship.

2. (5 minutes) A student reads the timeline out loud so that everyone gets a sense of when David lived. Then a student reads the introduction. Discuss: What motivated David to arrange for Uriah to be killed?

3. (10 minutes) Students read the debate in pairs, with one person playing David and the other playing Nathan. Then, the pair answers the first three questions in "Cross Examination."

4. (5 minutes) Discuss: How did Nathan confront David? What did Nathan do so that David would be more likely to listen to him? What led David to admit that he was wrong?

5. (5 minutes) Write the phrase *ometz lev* on the board and translate it. How did Nathan demonstrate *ometz lev?* Then write the phrase *lo talech rachil b'amecha* on the board and translate it. Did Nathan violate the prohibition of revealing secrets? Why or why not?

Wrapping It Up: (5 minutes)

In pairs, share a situation where you confronted someone and gave him or her criticism. How did the person react? Did you try to formulate your criticism in a helpful way? How? Was there any way you could have expressed your criticism in a more helpful way?

David and Nathan, Lesson 2

Essential Question: When must we stand up to authority and express our convictions?

Lesson Objectives: Students will be able to:

1. Explain why Nathan stood up and confronted David.

2. Formulate arguments outlining when it is necessary to blow the whistle on corruption.

3. Identify situations in their own lives where they can stand up to authority to express their own convictions.

Getting Started: (5 minutes)

If you were Nathan, what concerns might you have about confronting King David? Why would you confront him? What risks would you face? In pairs, students debate—from Nathan's perspective—whether or not to confront David, with one student presenting arguments in favor and one student presenting arguments against.

Exploring the Text:

1. (10 minutes) Read together "Debate It" and then consider the following real-life scenario. In December 2005, *The New York Times* published an article claiming:

   Months after the Sept. 11 attacks, President Bush secretly authorized the National Security Agency to eavesdrop on Americans and others inside the United States to search for evidence of terrorist activity without the court-approved warrants ordinarily required for domestic spying, according to government officials.

   The United States government, according to the article, read emails and monitored telephone calls inside the United States in order to uncover terrorist activity. *The New York Times* waited a year to publish the article (See http://www.nytimes.com/2005/12/16/politics/16program.html?pagewanted=all), because President Bush had pleaded with them not to publish the story. Government officials worried that publishing the information would alert terrorists to the government's activity and compromise national security.

2. (10 minutes) In pairs, students write arguments for and against publishing the New York Times article. Students may use the Internet for research if they wish. Then answer the question: Would you have published the *New York Times* article? Why or why not?

3. (15 minutes) **Experiential Learning:** Students write a "Letter to the Editor" to their school, town, or local Jewish newspaper discussing a problem in their community that they believe needs to be talked about and acted on. The letter could voice a protest of a school or town policy, point out how your community is not meeting the needs of (or discriminating against) a particular group or certain individuals within your community, or criticize the leadership of the community's actions in a certain situation.

Wrapping It Up: (5 minutes)

Those students who wish to summarize their letters to the editor for the class may do so. Discuss the questions: Why do you believe that the cause you discussed in your letter is important? Why does the particular problem motivate you to find the courage (*ometz lev*) to confront authority?

Ben Zakkai and the Zealots, Lesson 1

Essential Question: When is it justified for a nation to go to war?

Lesson Objectives: Students will be able to:

1. Give reasons that may justify a nation going to war.

2. Explain why the Zealots wanted to go to war against the Romans and why the moderates opposed them.

3. Define the values of *rodef shalom* and *milchemet chovah* and explain how they come into play in the debate between the Zealots and the moderates.

Getting Started: (5 minutes)

When is it justified for a nation to go to war? Brainstorm with the class and write down a list of reasons to go to war that the students feel are just. If students are having trouble thinking of reasons, ask them about wars in recent history that they feel were just and why.

Exploring the Text:

1. (10 minutes) Write the years of the timeline on pieces of paper and hang them up in order on the wall so that the students can stand next to them. Write each of the different events on the timeline on slips of paper (some years include more than one event, so write these on separate slips), and hand these out to the students. Each student, with the help of the class, tries to stand next to the proper year. At the end, make sure the students are standing next to the correct years.

2. (5 minutes) Student reads the introduction out loud. Imagine you are a Jewish resident of Jerusalem living in the year 66 C.E. Would you fight with Abba Sikra or be a pacifist like Ben Zakkai? Why?

3. (5 minutes) In pairs, students act out the debate and summarize each side's arguments.

4. (5 minutes) As a class, discuss: What values motivate each side? Read "Competing Values" together.

5. (15 minutes) **Experiential Learning:** Invite someone who is currently serving or has recently served in the Israeli or American army to come speak to the class. Ask the guest to share his or her reasons for joining the army. When does he or she feel that the use of military force is justified? When is the use of force excessive?

Wrapping It Up: (5 minutes)

Students respond in writing to the following questions: What did you learn from the soldier's words? What surprised you? Under what circumstances would you enlist to fight for your country or Israel? (See "Reflections.")

Ben Zakkai and the Zealots, Lesson 2

Essential Question: How far are we willing to go in order to defeat our enemies?

Lesson Objectives: Students will be able to:

1. Explain why the Zealots argued that "we must fight the Romans at all costs" and why the moderates opposed this argument.

2. Describe the Torah's approach to war.

3. Formulate their own positions regarding what means of warfare are justified in order to defeat the enemy.

Getting Started: (5 minutes)

Abba Sikra states that, "We must fight the Romans at all costs. If it takes starving our countrymen to make them fight, so be it." Even if you accept Abba Sikra's argument that we must fight the Romans, do you agree that we must do so at all costs? Is it right to starve our countrymen in order to make them fight? Do the ends in this case justify the means? Why or why not? Explain that a Zealot means an extremist, and Abba Sikra is advocating extreme means to fight the Romans.

Exploring the Text:

1. (10 minutes) In pairs, read Deuteronomy 20:5-20, and write a list of rules about going to war that you find in the passage.

2. (10 minutes) As a class, discuss: Is the approach to war in Deuteronomy similar to that of the Zealots or that of Ben Zakkai? Why? Read the section "Debate It" together, and debate the question: Do you agree with the Torah's approach? Why or why not?

3. (15 minutes) **Experiential Learning:** Split into small groups. Each small group creates its own list of rules for going to war—rules they believe are as just as possible. The rules should include guidelines for how to enlist soldiers to fight, how to treat the enemy during battle, and how to treat the enemy after battle if your side is victorious. Each group writes their rules on a posterboard. When the students are done, they may go around the room to look at the other groups' work.

Wrapping It Up: (5 minutes)

In pairs, read "What Would You Do?" together, and discuss what your answer to the question would be. In deciding on an answer, think about the Torah's understanding of just war, and your small group's discussion of rules of war.

Hillel and Shammai, Lesson 1

Essential Question: Is Torah law eternal and unchanging, or does it develop to accommodate changes over time?

Lesson Objectives: Students will be able to:

1. Explain the debate between the Pharisees and the Sadducees.

2. Define *Torah min hashamayim* and *Torah she b'al-peh.*

3. Reflect on their own beliefs regarding *Torah min hashamayim* and *Torah she b'al-peh.*

Getting Started: (10 minutes)

The Torah states that, "If anyone maims someone else, as he has done so shall it be done to him: fracture for fracture, eye for eye, tooth for tooth. The injury he inflicted on another shall be inflicted on him" (Leviticus 24:19-20). Ask: What do these verses mean?

The rabbis interpret this passage as saying that the injurer must give the injured person the monetary worth of his eye or tooth, rather than literally have his eye poked out or his tooth pulled. Discuss: Do you think the rabbis' interpretation reflects the original intention of the Torah verses? If not, what do you think motivated the rabbis to interpret the verses as they did? If you were a judge and you needed to apply these verses today, how would you interpret the verses? Why?

Exploring the Text:

1. (10 minutes) In pairs, read the introduction, and answer questions #1 and #2 of "Clarification."

2. (5 minutes) Explain that while both the Pharisees and the Sadducees believe in *Torah min hashamayim,* they disagree regarding *Torah she b'al-peh.* The Pharisees believe in *Torah she b'al-peh* and are actively involved in developing it, whereas the Sadducees reject it. How would the Pharisees interpret the verses in Leviticus above? How would the Sadducees interpret them?

3. (5 minutes) Brainstorm as a class advantages and disadvantages of the Pharisees' and the Sadducees' different approaches.

4. (10 minutes) **Experiential Learning:** All students stand up and go to the front of the room. The teacher reads a statement, and the students go to one side of the room if they agree and the other side of the room if they disagree. If the students are undecided or partially agree, they can stand somewhere in between the two sides. After the students find their places, ask some students to explain their views. Students can also ask each other questions based on where they are standing.

   Statements include:

   - If I were living at that time, I would be a Pharisee.

   - I believe in *Torah min hashamayim.*

   - I believe that *Torah she b'al-peh* has authority over me.

   - Only the rabbis have the authority to interpret Torah laws.

   - I decide which Torah laws are relevant to my life and which are not.

Wrapping It Up: (5 minutes)

Each student writes a paragraph beginning with "I believe …" that explains what he or she believes regarding the questions above and why.

Hillel and Shammai, Lesson 2

Essential Question: Should we interpret Torah laws strictly, or allow other factors, such as compassion for others, to influence our interpretation of the law?

Lesson Objectives: Students will be able to:

1. Identify factors that may influence how a person interprets the law.

2. Describe Hillel and Shammai's different approaches to Jewish law.

3. Reflect on their own approaches to interpreting Torah law.

Getting Started: (5 minutes)

Brainstorm with the class a list of factors that may affect how a judge interprets the law (*personal values, politics, religious beliefs, race or ethnicity, compassion, the time and place in which the judge lives, etc.*) Remind the students of the rabbis' interpretation of "eye for an eye" and ask what factors affected the rabbis' interpretation of the biblical verses.

Exploring the Text:

1. (10 minutes) Read "The Great Debate" as a class. Discuss: What lies behind each of Hillel and Shammai's positions? Based on Hillel and Shammai's positions in each of the three debates, how would you describe each of their approaches to interpreting the law? What factors motivate each person's rulings? Do you agree with Hillel or Shammai's approach and why?

2. (5 minutes) In pairs, discuss question #2 in "Cross Examination." Do you think it is possible to interpret a law impartially, without allowing one's socio-economic status or other details of one's personal life (politics, religion, moral values, etc.) to affect how one interprets the law? Is doing so an ideal to strive for? Why or why not?

3. (10 minutes) As a class, read "Echoes from the Past" and discuss: Do you agree with Rabbi Judah Ha-Nasi's ruling (the lenient group) or the strict ruling? Why? Is Rabbi Judah Ha-Nasi's approach more similar to Hillel's or Shammai's? Why?

4. (15 minutes) **Experiential Learning:** Each student chooses an issue of Jewish law that he or she feels strongly about, and writes a *teshuva* (Jewish legal ruling) as if s/he were a rabbi who is a leader of the Jewish community. In the *teshuva,* the rabbi must either reinterpret Jewish law to accommodate the needs of the Jewish community today, or defend the traditional interpretation of Jewish law even though it may be difficult to follow today. Issues may include: patrilineal descent, women becoming rabbis, or prohibiting smoking. Students may research the topic on the Internet.

Wrapping It Up: (5 minutes)

In pairs, students share their *teshuvot.* Discuss: Did you interpret Jewish law leniently, like Hillel, or strictly, like Shammai? What factors influenced your interpretation of Jewish law?

Hillel and Shammai, Lesson 3

Essential Question: Should we strive to understand American constitutional law according to its original intent, or interpret it to accommodate changing times?

Lesson Objectives: Students will be able to:

1. Explain the originalist argument in American constitutional law.

2. Provide examples of cases in American law where judges use the originalist argument.

3. Compare and contrast the debate today about originalism with the Hillel v. Shammai and the Sadducees v. Pharisees debates.

Getting Started: (5 minutes)

Discuss question #3 in "Clarification." Explain that today in the United States, we use the term "originalist" to describe judges who refuse to interpret laws in ways that were not intended when the law first appeared. In the two legal debates we looked at so far, who is closest to the "originalist" position—the Pharisees or the Sadducees? Hillel or Shammai?

Exploring the Text:

1. (5 minutes) As a class, read "Debate It." Explain that each pair will research (using the Internet) a different question in American constitutional law in which "originalists" and their opponents debate how to apply the law. Give a list of constitutional questions, and each pair chooses a question. If a particular pair wants to research a question not included on the list, they may do so with the teacher's approval. The list may include:

   • Gun control (Printz v. United States; District of Columbia v. Heller)

   • Affirmative action (Gratz v. Bollinger)

   • Regulating the sale of violent video games to children (Brown v. Entertainment Merchants Association)

   • Corporate spending on behalf of political candidates (Citizens United v. Federal Election Commission)

   • Lethal injection as a means of execution (Baze v. Rees)

   Depending on the research abilities of the class, the teacher may want to hand out short paragraphs summarizing the Constitutional question and the originalist position on that question.

2. (20 minutes) **Experiential Learning:** Each pair researches its topic and writes a list of arguments for and against, including the originalist argument. Students then create posters (by hand or on the computer) to hang in the school that will educate the student population about the particular issues researched. Posters may also advocate for a particular position.

3. (10 minutes) In small groups of three or four pairs each, pairs share their posters. What is the originalist argument in your case? Do you agree with the argument? Each small group should include only one pair researching a given topic.

Wrapping It Up: (5 minutes)

As a class, discuss: Do you agree with the originalist position for interpreting the Constitution? What do you think the Sadducees, Pharisees, Hillel, and Shammai would say about the originalist argument were they alive today? Is your approach to interpreting Torah law similar or different than your approach to interpreting the Constitution? Why?

The Vilna Gaon and the Ba'al Shem Tov, Lesson 1

Essential Question: Is Torah study or joyful prayer the best way to connect to God?

Lesson Objectives: Students will be able to:

1. Provide examples of different ways to connect to God.

2. Describe the debate between the Ba'al Shem Tov and the Vilna Gaon.

3. Define *Talmud Torah* and *simcha* and explain how each can be a spiritual path.

Getting Started: (10 minutes)

Each student writes for five minutes about a personal experience when he or she felt close to God (or for those who do not believe in God, about a personal spiritual experience). The students should write without stopping to think, and try to capture as many details of the experience as they can. Those students who wish to may share their experience with the class.

Exploring the Text:

1. (5 minutes) Brainstorm with the class: Based on the previous exercise, what are different ways that people connect to God? *(prayer, nature, family, Torah)* Write a list on the board.

2. (10 minutes) In pairs, read the introduction together and answer questions #1 - #3 in "Clarification." For question #3, a hint can be to look at the three paragraphs of the Sh'ma: *v'ahavta, v'haya im shamoa,* and *vayomer.*

3. (5 minutes) As a class, read the time line, and then discuss question #5 in "Clarification." Why did Hasidism begin at this particular time in history?

4. (5 minutes) In the same pairs, act out the debate between the Ba'al Shem Tov and the Vilna Gaon, using the script. Then continue the argument in your own words.

5. (10 minutes) **Experiential Learning:** As a class, visit the synagogue library. Explain that the synagogue library can be a great place to help students do their own Torah study, as the Vilna Gaon advocates. Each student takes out a book on any Torah topic that interests him or her. The students' homework is to set aside time before the next lesson to study the Torah topic that interests them, either by reading part of the book on their own or by studying with a partner *(chevruta)* such as a parent or friend from the class.

Wrapping It Up: (5 minutes)

Introduce the values *Talmud Torah* and *simcha.* How do the Ba'al Shem Tov and the Vilna Gaon relate to each value? What are their arguments in favor of each one as a spiritual path? What arguments would you add to their arguments? Explain that through their homework assignment, the students will get a taste of *Talmud Torah,* the Vilna Gaon's path to God, and in the next lesson, the students will get a taste of *simcha,* the Ba'al Shem Tov's path to God.

The Vilna Gaon and the Ba'al Shem Tov, Lesson 2

Essential Question: How can I cultivate awareness of God in my life?

Lesson Objectives: Students will be able to:

1. Reflect on their personal experience studying Torah as a way to connect to God.

2. Experience what it means to try to connect to God through nature.

3. Provide examples of ways they can cultivate spiritual awareness in their own lives.

Getting Started: (5 minutes)

Discuss: If you were living in that time, do you think you would be a follower of the Ba'al Shem Tov or the Vilna Gaon? Why? Which spiritual approach do you prefer? Explain that in this class, we will try to understand for ourselves the spiritual path that each person advocates.

Exploring the Text:

1. (5 minutes) In pairs, discuss: What was your experience of *Talmud Torah* at home this week like? Was it spiritual, intellectually interesting, or boring? Do you ever find Torah study (whether it be at Hebrew School, at home, in camp, or in the synagogue) inspiring? When and why? Is it ever difficult for you to be inspired by Torah study? Why?

2. (20 minutes) Explain that while all of you have studied Torah, as the Vilna Gaon emphasizes, some of you may not have tried to connect to God in nature, as the Ba'al Shem Tov suggests. Take the class outside, to the nearest place where the students can spread out and be in nature. (If this is impossible at your school, you can also give this exercise as an assignment for home.) Explain that one of the ways to connect to God in Hasidism is *hitbodedut,* in which a person goes out in nature and talks to God. The students' assignment is to talk out loud to God (a whisper is sufficient, so long as they are vocalizing the words) about whatever is on their mind. The idea is to keep talking without stopping. If the student does not believe in God or has questions about God, he or she can talk about those questions and doubts.

3. (10 minutes) Gather the students and return to the classroom. Ask those students who wish to share something about their experience. How did you feel trying to talk to God? What was difficult about the exercise? What did you learn from the experience?

Wrapping It Up: (5 minutes)

Students answer in writing the last question in "Reflections." What can you do to cultivate an awareness that God is all around you? (Or, for those students who do not believe in God, what can you do to cultivate spirituality in your life?) What can you learn from the Ba'al Shem Tov and/or the Vilna Gaon about how to create more spiritual moments in your life? Do your best to list concrete examples of steps you can take (*spend some time alone in nature each week, make a time to study Torah with a partner, go to youth services at the synagogue*).

Spinoza and the Amsterdam Rabbis, Lesson 1

Essential Question: What must someone believe and/or do (if anything) in order to be a member of the Jewish community?

Lesson Objectives: Students will be able to:

1. Consider different criteria for membership in the Jewish community.

2. Understand the historical context of the Converso community in 17th century Amsterdam.

3. Explain why the rabbis excommunicated Spinoza.

Getting Started: (5 minutes)

Discuss: What do you do or believe that makes you part of the Jewish community? *(attend synagogue, participate in Jewish family events, go to Hebrew school)* What do you do that distances yourself from the Jewish community? (See "Reflections").

Exploring the Text:

1. (10 minutes) **Experiential Learning:** Divide the students into small groups. Each group builds its ideal Jewish community, using different colored modeling clay. Each group answers the questions: Who is part of your Jewish community? Are there any membership requirements? *(someone who is born to a Jewish mother and/or father, someone who affiliates with Jewish institutions such as a synagogue, JCC, or school, someone who believes in God and/or the Torah)* What do you do together as a community? Are there any behaviors or beliefs that would exclude a member from your community? *(convert to another religion, take on the practices or beliefs of another religion such as Buddhist meditation or belief in Jesus, not circumcise one's son, make anti-Semitic comments publicly, do something that endangers your community)*

2. (10 minutes) Each group shares their model with the class. Discuss: How did you decide who should be part of your community? Were there disagreements? About what? How did you resolve them?

3. (5 minutes) Ask students: What is the Inquisition? *(a Roman Catholic tribunal to discover and punish heresy, often directed at converts to Catholicism suspected of insincerity)* Who are the Conversos? *(Jews in medieval Spain during the time of the Inquisition who converted to Christianity in order to escape death, many of whom continued to practice Judaism secretly)* Would you still consider them part of the Jewish community? Read the timeline together to provide context for the debate.

4. (10 minutes) In pairs, read the introduction and answer "Clarification" questions #1, #2, and #4.

Wrapping It Up: (5 minutes)

Discuss as a class: If you were one of the Amsterdam rabbis, would you have excommunicated Spinoza? Ask for a show of hands. Why or why not? What are the advantages and disadvantages of excommunicating him? Emphasize that failing to excommunicate Spinoza could endanger the livelihood of the entire Amsterdam Jewish community. Would Spinoza be excommunicated from the Jewish community today? See the last question in "Clarification."

Spinoza and the Amsterdam Rabbis, Lesson 2

Essential Question: How can we balance individual freedom with the good of the community in our lives and our society?

Lesson Objectives: Students will be able to:

1. Define *bechirah chofsheet* and *kehilah* and explain how the two values may conflict.

2. Describe Spinoza's beliefs and explain how he related to these values.

3. Provide real life examples where the two values conflict.

Getting Started: (5 minutes)

Discuss: Have you ever made a personal sacrifice in order to be a part of a community? What?

Exploring the Text:

1. (10 minutes) In pairs, read "The Great Debate" and rewrite it in modern day-to-day simple English (feel free to include slang). Use the dictionary to look up any words you don't understand.

2. (5 minutes) Discuss: What did Spinoza believe that was different than the traditional Jewish views at the time (and the views of the rabbis of Amsterdam)? What do you think of his beliefs? Do you think that those beliefs should not be allowed in the Jewish community?

3. (5 minutes) Read together "Competing Values." Ask: What are some examples of individual rights or freedoms that have been debated in recent years in the United States? *right to bear arms, gay rights, abortion rights, euthanasia—the patient's right to terminate his or her life in order to end suffering, right to health care)* Students can read "What Would You Do?" to themselves to get them thinking.

4. (15 minutes) **Experiential Learning:** Each student (or pair of students) chooses one of the above debates about particular individual rights or freedoms to research. Students summarize the arguments for either side, making sure to identify arguments relating to the common good and/or individual freedoms. Each student writes a letter to a local politician advocating a particular view on these questions.

Wrapping It Up: (5 minutes)

Those students who wish to present their issue to the class and explain their position may do so. Ask: Do you advocate for *bechirah chofsheet* in this case? Why or why not? What is the place of communal values (values of the *kehilah*) in your position and why?

Geiger, Hirsch, and Frankel, Lesson 1

Essential Question: How does Judaism develop to reflect changing times?

Lesson Objectives: Students will be able to:

1. Explain how historical events influence the development of Judaism.

2. Understand the historical context of the emergence of denominations in Judaism.

3. Identify the advantages and disadvantages of changing Jewish practice in order to accommodate the changing times and places in which Jews live.

Getting Started: (5 minutes)

How do you and your family practice Judaism differently than your grandparents? Than your great-grandparents? How do you imagine your great-grandparents' great-grandparents might have practiced Judaism? Why do you think you do things differently? What historical events influenced the changes in Jewish practice over the generations?

Exploring the Text:

1. (10 minutes) **Experiential Learning:** Students prepare to interview their parents and grandparents, or other elders in their family, to find out how their Jewish practices and beliefs were different than Jewish practices today. Each student writes a list of questions that he or she will ask. Students may use the Internet to learn more about Jewish life where their families come from, in order to provide a context for their interview and think of appropriate questions. If possible, students should record their interviews. When the interviews are completed, students can share them with the class online or in the classroom.

2. (5 minutes) Students divide into pairs. Each pair reads the introduction and answers questions #1, #2, and #3 in "Clarification."

3. (5 minutes) Discuss as a class: Do you identify more with Elke's father or mother? Why? Do you think changing Jewish practices can lead to assimilation and "destroy our sacred tradition"? Why or why not?

4. (10 minutes) Divide the students into four small groups. Each group receives one of the first four events on the timeline. The group must answer the questions: What happened at your point in the timeline? How do you think this event changed what Jews believed and how Jews practiced Judaism?

5. (10 minutes) Each group presents its answers to the whole class. The class reads the rest of the timeline. Ask: How do you think the four events you studied influenced the emergence of the different denominations?

Wrapping It Up: (5 minutes)

Each student writes a paragraph from the perspective of his or her great-grandchild describing how he or she practices Judaism. Their writing should respond to the last question in "Reflections": What do you think Judaism will look like 100 years from now? What do you think will happen over the next 100 years that will influence Judaism? How?

Geiger, Hirsch, and Frankel, Lesson 2

Essential Question: How should we balance tradition and change in Judaism?

Lesson Objectives: Students will be able to:

1. Describe practices and beliefs of the founders of the different Jewish denominations.

2. Explain how each founder relates to changing Jewish traditions and why.

3. Reflect on their own practices and beliefs in relation to the denominations.

Getting Started: (5 minutes)

Write different quotes from "The Great Debate" on pieces of paper, and place the pieces of paper around the room. Each student walks around the room, reads the quotes, and stands next to the quote with which he most agrees. Point out to the students that all quotes relate to Judaism, the Jewish people, and Jewish law. If students have trouble understanding a quote, they should ask the teacher. Teachers should choose the quotes that are most relevant to their class. Quotes may include:

- Faith and reason are the guarantee for Judaism's survival.

- All laws and all prayers that are unworthy or irrelevant should be eliminated.

- Our slogan is 'moderate reform.' Time hurries onward and radical reforms are demanded, but we do not want to forget that not all demands of our times are justified.

- I believe that a part of the service must be held in English, but Hebrew must predominate. Our youth must be taught Hebrew in order to understand the service and the Bible.

- From now on, no distinction between duties for men and women should be made.

- To cut, curtail and obliterate the tenets and ordinances of Judaism—is that the reform we need? To remodel the Divine service in accordance with the demands of the age—is that the reform we desire?

Exploring the Text:

1. (15 minutes) While still standing in different spots throughout the room, students representing each quote read the quote, say it in their own words (teacher may need to help out here) and then explain why they agree with the quote. Students may ask each other questions based on where they are standing. At the end, those students who wish to may change places if they decide they agree with another quote more than the quote they initially chose. Explain that all these quotes represent the views of rabbis living in Germany in the 19th century, and these views became the basis of the Jewish denominations we know today: Reform, Conservative, and Orthodox.

2. (10 minutes) As a class, read "The Great Debate" together, with different students playing the three different rabbis. Ask: Were you surprised by which quotes belonged to which rabbis, given the movement they represent? Why? The class then responds to the third "Cross Examination" question.

continues...

Geiger, Hirsch, and Frankel, Lesson 2, continued

3. (15 minutes) **Experiential Learning:** Each student imagines that he or she is the founder of a new movement of Judaism particularly suited to the time and place in which we live. What are the fundamental beliefs and practices? What traditional beliefs and practices will you maintain and which will you change? What is the name of the movement? Create the homepage of your new movement's website (either on the computer or on paper). What is your movement's logo? What picture or pictures are on the page? What links? What are the headings for the different parts of the website?

Wrapping It Up: (5 minutes)

In pairs, share your website. Explain how you decided on which Jewish beliefs and practices would be fundamental to your movement, and particularly how you decided which traditions to maintain and which to change.

Geiger, Hirsch, and Frankel, Lesson 3

Essential Question: How can we reinterpret the covenant to be meaningful today?

Lesson Objectives: Students will be able to:

1. Define the values of *kitvei kodesh* and *am yisrael* and explain how they come into play in Jewish life today.

2. Describe how members of different Jewish denominations today reinterpret the covenant.

3. Reflect on how they reinterpret the covenant to be meaningful in their own lives.

Getting Started: (5 minutes)

Read "Competing Values" together as a class. Write *am yisrael* on one side of the board, and *kitvei kodesh* on the other side of the board. Students think of examples from their own Jewish life, from their family and/or their synagogue, that reflect one or the other of these values. (*Women leading prayer or wearing a kippah and tallit is one example of the value of am yisrael; saying the Sh'ma each day using the original words is an example of kitvei kodesh.*) Write each example on the board under the appropriate heading.

Exploring the Text:

1. (5 minutes) Read "Debate It" as a class. Each teacher invites about three people to speak to the class from different Jewish denominations. The speakers do not necessarily have to be leaders of the Jewish community—anyone who can speak articulately and openly about what he or she believes would be appropriate. The key is that the speakers represent a variety of views. Explain to the class that today we are inviting people to speak to our class who belong to different Jewish denominations and hold different views regarding the two values above—from the more traditionalist, to the more modernist, to somewhere in between. Describe briefly who will be on the panel.

2. (5 minutes) In pairs, students prepare questions to ask the speakers on the panel about their personal views regarding the history and values we have studied in this chapter. Students may read "Echoes from the Past" in order to get ideas for the kind of questions they may ask.

3. (30 minutes) **Experiential Learning:** The panel speaks to the class, using a question and answer format. Each pair can ask at least one of their questions. The teacher should feel free to ask any central questions that the students do not address. Make sure to emphasize the question of how each of the speakers interprets the covenant to be meaningful to him or her as a Jew living in the United States today.

Wrapping It Up: (5 minutes)

Students answer the following questions in writing: What did the panelists say that most made them think? Did they agree or disagree with the panelist and why? Answer the first question in "Reflections."

Herzl and Wise, Lesson 1

Essential Question: Do the Jews need a Jewish state?

Lesson Objectives: Students will be able to:

1. Describe the historical context in which Herzl founded the Zionist movement.

2. Make arguments for and against establishing a Jewish state.

3. Articulate their own positions regarding whether the Jews need a Jewish state.

Getting Started: (10 minutes)

Present the following pairs of statements to the class, either verbally or via a PowerPoint presentation. After reading each statement and its opposing statement, students vote by a show of hands on which statement they agree with more. Then students defend each statement.

- I can be just as good a Jew living in the United States as living in Israel.
- I can be the best Jew possible only living in Israel.
- For me, being Jewish is mainly a religious identity.
- For me, being Jewish is mainly a national identity.
- Anti-Semitism will always be a danger to Jews living outside of Israel.
- Jews can live outside of Israel without being worried about anti-Semitism.
- Mixing Judaism with politics corrupts both Judaism and politics.
- Judaism can only be fully realized when it is applied to all parts of our lives, including politics.

Explain that in the next three lessons, we will explore the ideas underlying these statements.

Exploring the Text:

1. (5 minutes) Read the introduction together as a class. Discuss: Why did witnessing the Dreyfus trial lead Herzl to conclude that the Jews need a Jewish state?

2. (10 minutes) In pairs, answer questions #2, #3, and #4 in "Clarifications." Discuss: Do you think Herzl would have founded the Zionist movement if he were an American Jew?

3. (5 minutes) Read the timeline together as a class, making sure the students understand the key people, events, and ideas. Explain that your assignment will be to write a resolution regarding the Jewish state just as Rabbi Wise did.

4. (15 minutes) **Experiential Learning:** Each student receives the following assignment. Imagine you were a Jew living in the United States at the end of the 19th century. Would you support the Zionist movement? Why or why not? Write your own resolution explaining your position regarding the Jewish state. When you are done, try to get signatures for your resolution from other students by convincing them of your argument.

Wrapping It Up: (5 minutes)

Drawing on the resolutions and the material in the sourcebook, brainstorm with the class a list of reasons that the Jews need a Jewish state and a list of reasons that the Jews do not need a Jewish state.

Herzl and Wise, Lesson 2

Essential Question: As an American Jew, what is my relationship to Israel?

Lesson Objectives: Students will be able to:

1. Explain Herzl and Rabbi Wise's opposing positions regarding Judaism and the Jewish state.

2. Define *l'umanut* and *dat hayahadut* and describe Herzl and Rabbi Wise's approaches to these values.

3. Explore their own relationship to Israel as American Jews.

Getting Started: (5 minutes)

Brainstorm with the class: What are different ways that American Jews can make Israel part of their lives? *(reading the news about Israel, including Israel in their prayers, visiting Israel, giving money to Israeli organizations, making aliyah, political advocacy on behalf of Israel. Note that voicing their critiques of Israel can also be a way for students to make Israel part of their lives; not all ways of relating to Israel are exclusively positive.)*

Exploring the Text:

1. (10 minutes) Read the debate as a class, with one student playing Herzl and one student playing Rabbi Wise, and other students serving as the "translators." After each statement of Herzl or Rabbi Wise, the "translator," with the help of the class, says the statement in simple English that the class can understand.

2. (5 minutes) In pairs, answer the following questions: What does Herzl see as uniting the Jewish people? *(anti-semitism)* What about Rabbi Wise? *(religion)* What do you see as uniting the Jewish people?

3. (5 minutes) Read "Competing Values" together as a class. Discuss: Based on your discussion in pairs, which element of Judaism does Herzl emphasize, and which element does Rabbi Wise emphasize? Which element of Judaism, religion or nationalism, is most important to you personally? Why?

4. (15 minutes) **Experiential Learning:** Explain that even though there is now a Jewish state, Herzl and Rabbi Wise's debate is still relevant to us, because the different values they emphasize shape how we, as American Jews, relate to Israel. Discuss: How does the way you define your Jewish identity affect how you relate to Israel? *(For example, if you see Judaism primarily as your religion, perhaps Israel is a place to go to for religious inspiration, whereas if you see Judaism as primarily your nationality, you may feel an obligation to support Israel as a country, through political advocacy or even serving in the army.)* Based on their answers to these questions, each student chooses a project for engaging with Israel that he or she can work on for the next couple of weeks that will be personally meaningful. Each student can use the Internet to research and begin working on the project. Examples of projects include:

   • Raising money for an Israeli organization that you personally support.

   • Writing a letter to your American government officials advocating on behalf of Israel.

   • Creating your own prayer to say regularly on behalf of Israel.

   • Reading the news about Israel each day and writing a brief news update to share with your class each time you meet.

   • Learning a new Hebrew word each day and thinking of fun ways to make the words you learn part of your classroom life.

Wrapping It Up: (5 minutes)

In pairs, students share their projects and explain why their projects are personally meaningful. Students may give suggestions to their partners about how to make their projects most effective.

Herzl and Wise, Lesson 3

Essential Question: What is the ideal relationship between religion and state in Israel?

Lesson Objectives: Students will be able to:

1. Explain why Rabbi Wise believed that Judaism and politics should not mix.
2. Make arguments for and against the separation of religion and state in Israel.
3. Articulate their own visions of the ideal relationship between religion and state in Israel.

Getting Started: (5 minutes)

Brainstorm a list of ways that Jewish religion shapes public life in Israel. *(Jewish religious political parties, the Rabbinate controlling all marriages, divorces, and conversions performed in Israel, celebrating Jewish holidays and studying the Bible in the public school system, public transportation closing on the Sabbath, all army bases serving only kosher food, Sabbath being the national day of rest, the national anthem and national flag using Jewish religious themes).* Do you think that the Jewish religion should affect public life in these ways? Why or why not?

Exploring the Text:

1. (5 minutes) As a class, answer questions #3 and #4 in "Cross Examination." What would Rabbi Wise think about the ways the Jewish religion shapes public life in Israel today?

2. (10 minutes) In pairs, read "Debate It" and debate the question of whether the Law of Return should include those who converted in a non-Orthodox conversion or not. Assign each partner one side of the debate. Then switch.

3. (5 minutes) As a class, discuss: How would you define a Jew for the purposes of the Law of Return? *(anyone who identifies as a Jew, anyone who has Jewish ancestry, anyone who converts in a formal conversion ceremony)* Or, would you abolish the Law of Return altogether in favor of an immigration policy that does not take religion into account?

4. (5 minutes) Explain that the question of who is a Jew in Israel is relevant not only to who is included in the Law of Return, but also to how Israeli citizens are registered on their identity cards, and whether or not an Israeli citizen can get married in Israel. The answer to the question of who is a Jew according to Israeli law may be different in each of these situations. See the "Case Study," where the Supreme Court defines a Reform convert as Jewish for the purposes of how she is registered on her identity card.

5. (15 minutes) In small groups, each group discusses what it sees as the ideal relationship between religion and state in Israel, addressing some of the questions discussed in the textbook and at the beginning of today's class. Each group creates a poster, diorama, or collage representing what it sees as the ideal relationship between religion and state. When each group is done, it can go around to the other groups and look at their work. Students may wish to display their work in the school.

Wrapping It Up: (5 minutes)

As a class, discuss: How did your group decide what to do? Did members of your group disagree? How did you resolve those disagreements? Were there members of the group who wanted to leave your group because they did not support the final product? Explain that in Israel, many different kinds of Jews (who are much more different from one another than the members of your group) live together and try to figure out how to build a state that best encompasses their different values. The question of the relationship between religion and state is hotly debated in Israeli society, as Israelis struggle to define the nature of the Jewish state.